Dear Reader

365 Empowering Ways to Move Beyond Abuse

A Daily Healing Companion for Survivors

Healing is possible!
Some ways to do so are

by

Moriah S. St. Clair

in your hands right now
I wish you Peace

Blessings

Pathways United Publications

365 Empowering Ways to Move Beyond Abuse

A Daily Healing Companion for Survivors

by Moriah S. St. Clair

Published by

Pathways United Publications
P. O. Box 7031 • Corte Madera, CA 94976 USA
www.pathwaysunited.com

Editor: Myra J. Bicknell
Cover Design: Moriah S. St. Clair • Cover Artist: Gary A. Fox

Library of Congress Catalog Card Number: 00-91047
St. Clair, Moriah S.
    365 Empowering Ways to Move Beyond Abuse:
    A Daily Healing Companion for Survivors
    1. Child abuse 362.7'04   2. Recovery
    3. Self-actualization/Self-help

ISBN: 1-892268-04-3

Printed in the United States of America
Printed on acid-free recycled paper

First printing, year 2000
    10 9 8 7 6 5 4 3 2 1

What People are Saying About this Book

"Superlative. Outstanding. There are not enough adjectives to properly describe Moriah S. St. Clair's *365 Empowering Ways to Move Beyond Abuse*. What an exquisite roadmap to recovery. Each chapter catapults you to a new spiritual realm. This wonderful book is imperative for survivors of child abuse or for any person who may be seeking a better quality or meaning of life. The benefits from this simple and spiritual formula for a healthy life are enormous."—*Claire R. Reeves, President, Founder, and CEO of Mothers Against Sexual Abuse (MASA)*

"Overcoming the abuse I suffered took years. A seemingly endless journey to become whole and strong. If I had only had a copy of this book, I would have realized inspiration, hope, and healing much sooner. Its practical steps to recovery makes moving beyond abuse manageable. I will recommend this book to victims everywhere I speak."—*Tonya Flynt-Vega, Author of Hustled My Journey from Fear to Faith, Founder of The Tonya Flynt Foundation Against Pornography and Sexual Abuse, and Daughter of Larry Flynt (Hustler Magazine Publisher)*

"A practical and effective manual for crises of the heart. A gem for all of us." —*Walter Semkiw, M.D., Author*

"Excellent...very enabling tool as daily thoughts and as a quick reference on the healing journey."—*Judith Little, President of VOICES in Action, Inc. (Victims Of Incest Can Emerge Survivors)*

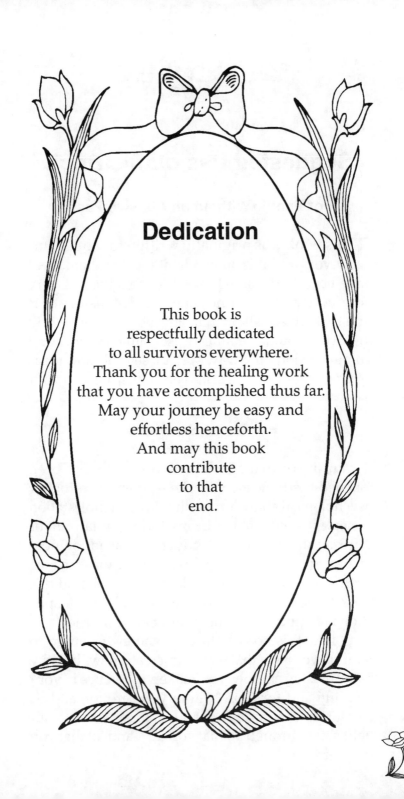

Dedication

This book is
respectfully dedicated
to all survivors everywhere.
Thank you for the healing work
that you have accomplished thus far.
May your journey be easy and
effortless henceforth.
And may this book
contribute
to that
end.

Suggested Use of this Book

For People Without an Abusive Past:

This book was originally written for abuse survivors and it is an excellent tool for them. Yet I have been told that 80 to 90% of this book is very helpful to people without an abusive history. It is true that we are all on a life journey of growth and discovery—and we all can use some support and guidance along the way. May these tools and ideas bring greater joy, peace, and empowerment to your path.

For Abuse Survivors:

If your life or that of someone you know has been touched by domestic violence—physical, verbal or psychological abuse—rape, incest, child molestation or neglect—elder abuse in any form—ritual, cult or spiritual abuse—deep or sudden loss, abandonment or betrayal—traumas of war, brainwashing or torture—or other acts of violence, you will find this book to be a very supportive, helpful, and inspirational companion along your healing journey.

Take this book with you wherever you go to remind yourself that you can create new, healthy patterns, stay empowered, make a difference in your own life and for those whom you care for, and be comfortable with yourself and others as you let your light shine through all that you do—and all that you truly are.

Table of Contents

Foreword
Preface
Author's Note

Foreword

This is the instruction manual that will enable you to improve your life by at least 1% a day for the rest of your life. If you diligently follow the suggestions in this book, at the end of a year you might expect a 365% improvement in your life. When you consider the compounding effects of all of these positive practices, you can expect even more. If we use the analogy of compound interest, the results in your life could amount to a 3700% improvement in one year. I recommend that you read this book. And, above all, I recommend that you implement the ideas every day of your life.

Jeffrey Mishlove, PhD
Licensed Clinical Psychologist
President, Intuition Network
Host, *Virtual U*, daily program on the
Wisdom Radio Network

Warning — Disclaimer

This book is intended to provide information in regard to the subject matter covered. It is sold with the understanding that the publisher, author, and bookseller are not engaged in rendering legal, medical, psychological or other professional services. If legal, medical, psychological or other such expert assistance is required, the services of a competent professional should be promptly sought.

You are urged to obtain and review other available material on the subject, consult with professionals in the field, and formulate your own opinions and decisions. For more information, inquire at your local library, bookstore, social services and referral agencies listed in your phone directory or contact a competent professional in the associated fields.

Any suggestions or information from this book which are implemented (in whole or in part or in conjunction with any other suggestion, information or act) shall be at the sole discretion and responsibility of you, the reader. Any true memory retrieval or "false memory" experience, assumptions made about yourself or others, and any physical, emotional, mental, and/or spiritual reaction or response on your part to the book's contents, shall be the sole liability and responsibility of you, the reader.

The purpose of this book is to share knowledge and insights gleaned from personal experiences of the author. The publisher, booksellers, and author shall have neither liability nor responsibility of any kind to any person or entity with respect to any change or stasis of any physical, emotional, mental, and/or spiritual state, or for any pain, suffering, loss or damage caused, or alleged to be caused, directly or indirectly by the contents of this book.

If you, the reader, do not wish to be bound by the above statements and conditions, then do not read beyond this page. You may return this book, unused, together with your receipt from place of its purchase, to the publisher for a full refund.

Preface

Healing involves numerous components:

- acknowledging your thoughts, feelings, and experiences

- releasing your emotions, judgments, and beliefs that are not supportive of your true being

- honoring and pacing your process

- willingness, courage, understanding, and patience

- accepting the hidden gifts and lessons found in the suffering

- grieving, forgiveness, compassion, and acting upon your new awareness

Ultimately healing involves the recognition and expression of your True Self.

Author's Note

All quotations in this book are from the book *Abused Beyond Words* by Moriah S. St. Clair. You may order a copy of this extraordinary, compelling true story —a 469 page book full of information, insights, and compassion—by purchasing it at your local bookstore, using the order form at the back of this book or by using the other options listed on that page.

Healing Steps

> *"Healing requires courage, clarity, patience, tolerance, and willingness to let go of our current perspective to make way for peace and joy. At times along the healing journey we may think that we do not possess the qualities or abilities that will transform us. And yet, it just may be that our personal trials and adversities exist for us to realize and call forth from within us the very qualities we once thought that we never could have." Page 411*

1 Commit to healing and moving beyond. Commitment propels you into action. It supports you with courage, strength, and stamina during rough times. It guarantees your success.

2 Acknowledge your abuse experience. You must first own what did happen before you can let it go. People who were not there have no right to deny your experience. People who were there and were abusive or were afraid to do anything to stop it are often too invested in maintaining the secret to tell the truth. Therefore it is up to you to acknowledge what happened.

3 Talk about your abuse experiences to willing listeners who are understanding, supportive, and compassionate. This will help you diffuse the pressure and emotional charge of having to hold it all by yourself. Communicate with a therapist, friend, clergyman, someone from a social services agency, co-participant in a peer-support group or an Internet chat room designed to support survivors.

4 Acknowledge your feelings. Considering the abuse that you experienced, it is perfectly natural for you to feel a range of feelings and different ones at different times. You may feel angry, enraged, sad, fearful, depressed, overwhelmed, betrayed, hopeless, disappointed, untrusting, needy, powerless, abandoned, lonely, empty, numb or feel nothing by being in denial of your pain. Emotions and feelings need acknowledgment and expression before their energies can be transformed into what you truly want to experience in life.

5 Release your emotions. This will help you to let go of the past and cope better in the present. You may need to indulge your emotions for a while to offset the suppression of them in early life. Then learn to manage them in a healthy way. In addition to therapy and talking to friends, there are many safe ways to surface and release your emotions. For example, imagine your abuser in a chair and say what you need to say to him or her. Or you can do an art project (even if you do not think that you are creative) to express how you feel. Scribble on a big pad using the colors you feel. Make a sculpture out of clay, then release your anger onto it by pounding it. Use a journal to write poetry, a letter to your abuser or dialogue with a specific part of yourself.

6 **Realize that it takes more energy to hold on than to let go.** Our resistance makes us feel tight and tired. Holding on is a way of avoiding the feelings that lay underneath. It actually creates more pain and strain. Letting go frees your energy to create and do what you want to do now.

7 **Redirect any displaced emotion or judgment back to where it belongs.** Rather than having general or global thoughts and feelings such as being mad at the whole world or all men or all of your family, ask yourself, "Who or what am I specifically or disappointed by or mad at?" Focusing in this way will help you acknowledge the source of your upset and help you feel justified in releasing it.

8 **Build tolerance to your feelings and the feelings of others.** The more you feel and express your feelings, the more comfortable you will be with them. Over time you will then expand and balance the range of feelings that you experience.

9 **Reduce your overwhelm.** Overwhelm is a signal that there are many emotions inside that you have not fully released. Ask yourself, "If I were not feeling overwhelmed right now, what would I be feeling instead?" This will generate awareness and expression of the specific feeling that really has been pressuring you. Deal with that one feeling.

10 **Focus on one thing or one small part of an experience at a time.** This will reduce your sense of overwhelm and make what you are facing feel more manageable so that you can work with it. You will feel a sense of accomplishment as you successfully face or resolve each piece.

15

11 **Give back the abusers' energy—their rage, hurt, shame, denial, etc.** As children and victims we tend to absorb the emotions from the abusers that they were not willing to feel themselves. By giving them back, you will feel lighter and be able to cope with your own emotional energy much better.

12 **Acknowledge the decisions and beliefs which you developed out of your experience.** At the time of the abuse you may have subconsciously or consciously made generalized decisions about yourself, men, women, the world, God, sex, touch, groups of people, and many other categories in order to protect yourself from future abuse. By owning your beliefs as your own decisions, you can realize that you have the power to re-evaluate and release beliefs that no longer support you. You then have the power to make new, healthy choices for yourself.

13 **Acknowledge the impact of the abuse on your life.** By seeing where the abuse and surrounding circumstances of the past affect you now, you can take charge to diffuse or disconnect those old issues and feelings from the truth of the present.

14 **Know that revisiting a memory, thought, or feeling is not backsliding.** You are actually experiencing another aspect or deeper level of the same issue. It is natural to deepen in awareness and perspective as you cultivate tolerance for more of the experience.

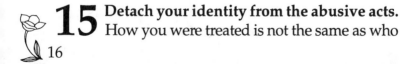

15 **Detach your identity from the abusive acts.** How you were treated is not the same as who you are. There is no point in holding on to that which is not the truth of your being. Repeat this statement to yourself often, "I am NOT my abuser's actions. I am who I am."

16 **Decide the following:** You can make new choices and let go of beliefs that no longer serve you. You don't need to let your abusers win by sabotaging your life now. Accept that it is YOUR life and you are in charge now.

17 **Think kind thoughts of yourself.** It is not supportive to judge or compare yourself to others. No one else has had your exact set of experiences, so their lives and responses will be different. Set achievable standards for yourself that do not pressure you. Consider all that you have overcome. Look at what you have achieved, what you give, and how you truly are. Positive thoughts will lift your spirits and strengthen your healing process.

18 **Be gentle with yourself.** You need to give yourself time and room to deal with issues from the past as well as the present. Give yourself nurturing experiences. You DO deserve them.

19 **Acknowledge other aspects of your being.** You are more than an abuse survivor. You have other interests, talents, relationships, work, a spiritual nature, contributions to the lives of others as well as your survivor skills. This awareness will bring balance and perspective to your life.

20 **Cultivate compassion toward others and your inner child.** In this way you can both assist others and transfer that ability back toward yourself. Think of someone you love right now. Shine loving light toward them. Feel that love. Now see yourself and shine that love toward you.

21 **Let go and grieve your past experience when you are ready.** Let go by grieving your childhood, your experiences, your old way of being, and potentials that have not yet blossomed. This will free up a lot of energy so that you can live more joyfully in the present rather than carrying around a dark cloud or heavy heart for the rest of your life.

22 **Let your grief pour out without judgment or reprisal.** Grief is facing your loss and allowing your feelings to be acknowledged and released. They will come out in layers in direct relationship to the supportiveness of your environment and the sense of security and trust you feel within. We must grieve our perceived loss before peace can be found.

23 **Be patient with your healing process.** Impatience signals that you are not wanting to be in the present situation or with your feelings or thoughts. Therefore patience yields acceptance.

24 **Take all the time you need to heal.** How much time? As much time as it takes for you. No one else can decide that for you. Everyone's set of experiences has its own unique combination of particular acts, duration, frequency, intensity, and responses to them. In addition, the circumstances surrounding the abuse may vary greatly. Did you live with the abuser(s)? Did you live with or know other victims? Did other adults protect you? Did they neglect your signals that something was wrong?

Was the abuse very violent or sadistic? Did you suppress memories of the abuse in order to cope? No two people's situations are exactly alike. Trust your own heart and soul's timetable.

25 **Get the message, lesson or awareness from the situation.** Ask yourself what knowledge, strength, talent, skill, perspective or way of being are you to be aware of and cultivate as a result of dealing with your abuse experiences.

26 **Act in accord with your new awareness.** Anchor your understanding in your daily life. Integrate your new awareness so that it becomes an active part of your life now.

Write Your Own Ideas Here

_____

_____

_____

_____

_____

_____

_____

_____

_____

_____

_____

_____

_____

_____

_____

_____

_____

_____

_____

_____

_____

_____

_____

_____

2

Reducing Stress

"Make realistic time goals relative to your constraints so that you can experience achievement, rather than induce pressure from unrealistic standards for your situation." Page 354

27 **Commune with nature.** Walk, run, exercise, sit, draw, paint, meditate, read, write, take photographs or rest by water, trees, grass, flowers or greenery. You will feel more at one with everything and get back to your natural self.

28 **Plan free time in advance.** This is a time in which you do not have to fulfill any obligations. This is your time to do with as you wish 100%. By planning ahead you can look forward to this time, balance your energy, and stay focused on current tasks because your playtime reward is in the foreseeable future.

29 **Treat yourself and your inner child to a fun activity.** Make a conscious choice to do something fun or entertaining to take a break from processing or coping with routine activities.

30 **Exercise or engage in a sport.** This will reduce tension in your muscles, release endorphins, and circulate energy throughout your body. When you feel better, you think better.

31 **Pray.** Ask for help, guidance, strength, relief, freedom or whatever you think will help you reduce the stress. Ask for help in identifying and dealing with the real underlying pressure.

32 **Meditate.** Calm your mind by quieting it and listening to a deeper truth within you. By placing your brainwave patterns in an alpha (rest) state through meditation, rather than a beta (active waking) state, you efficiently rejuvenate your body, mind, and spirit.

33 **Play peaceful, soothing music if you feel stressed and upbeat music if you feel stuck or depressed.** Without effort, your mind, emotions, and body will soon synchronize with the mellow or uplifting rhythms of the music you hear.

34 **Sing.** Whether you think that you can carry a tune or not, singing will help you get into the flow of what you are doing, rather than resisting it or feeling overwhelmed by it. Make up songs as you go along. Let yourself be silly. Have fun with it.

35 **Putter around the house, garden or garage.** This allows you to hang out without any pressure of accomplishing anything. You don't have to do anything in particular and you can do whatever you want. It is a great, relaxing way to ground and get reacquainted with your immediate surroundings, belongings, old fun projects, and self.

36 **Change locations.** Place yourself in a different atmosphere than what you have been living or working in. Take an hour or two and go to the beach, lake or stream. Take a walk on your lunch hour or bring your lunch to a nearby park. Take a day trip and drive through the countryside or explore a part of town that you do not usually visit. You will be better able to focus and cope upon return.

37 **Pretend you are a dog and bark or growl at seeming intruders.** This is more fun than a primal scream and can be just as effective. It can release tension. It may also help restore your sense of humor and perspective.

Write Your Own Ideas Here

_____

_____

_____

_____

_____

_____

3

Coping with Triggers

"...it is fascinating how the mind creatively attempts to remember what its conscious dimension has forgotten. We subconsciously put ourselves in all kinds of triggering situations until we become aware of that which we need to know." Page 249

38 **Have a special journal to write down the trigger when it happens.** The journal can "hold" the trigger for you until you have the support and time to explore what it is trying to help you remember, face, and feel. This frees you to relax in the moment, not be reactive, function in the present, and practice detaching from the trigger so that it loses power over you.

39 **Carry something soft with you to soothe your ruffled reactions to triggers, such as a smooth stone, silky cloth or cuddly teddy bear.** This will send your body, mind, and heart a new, safe, loving message to counteract the old upsetting message induced by the trigger. It can calm you and remind you of your new choices for your adult life.

40 **Breathe slowly and deeply.** Shallow breathing promotes feelings of powerlessness, fear, panic. Take command of your breathing and you take command of your feelings.

41 **Know that triggers are about the past, not the present.** Triggers help awaken memories and bring unresolved emotions to the surface. They exist to help you heal the past so that you can be empowered in the present.

42 **Ask the trigger to communicate to you what you are to learn, feel or release in your life now.** This will help you to move on to the message and purpose of the trigger, rather than stay in the pain or irritation of it. In this way, the trigger can diminish or completely dissolve in your life.

43 **Tell the trigger that it has no power over you anymore.** You can consciously choose to take back your power and energy from the trigger at any time. Remember, you live on a planet of free will.

44 **See what the trigger is reflecting or mirroring in your consciousness.** Triggers awaken our awareness of a belief, judgment or emotion that we are carrying which may require re-evaluation or healing.

45 **Reclaim your power.** Visualize the person, place, thing or situation that is triggering. Then identify your power sitting in that energy field. Tell the person, place, thing or situation, "This is my power and I am taking it back now. It belongs to

26

me." Visualize yourself taking your power back from the trigger. Visualize purifying that power in a way that is comfortable to you—in water, over fire, through sage smoke, etc. In this way, your power will have no residue from the trigger. Next, welcome your power home and absorb it into your psyche and body wherever it feels right for you. You may choose to pour it over your head or body, or take it in through your heart or another chakra. Then ask your power if it has any message for you. Listen, see or sense its response. Ask your power how you can support it to express itself in your life from now on. Act upon those answers.

Write Your Own Ideas Here

_____

_____

_____

_____

_____

_____

_____

_____

_____

_____

_____

_____

_____

_____

_____

_____

_____

_____

_____

_____

_____

_____

_____

_____

4

Embracing Painful Memories

"Sometimes we hide the truth from ourselves, only to rediscover it later as if it were something new entering our lives. Yet all the while we had been carrying it. First as an unknown burden, then as that which sets us free." Page 257

46 **Sort out your reactions to your memories and the circumstances resulting from those past events.** This will help you accept the reality of your past. Then you can work through your feelings and fallout from the experience with greater ease, confidence, and determination.

47 **Realize that our lives reflect many aspects of our consciousness.** We subconsciously put ourselves in all kinds of triggering situations until we become aware of that which we need to know or remember. Once you remember, grieve it.

48 **Use memories to update your thinking.** Memories point to where we made decisions, created beliefs, and stored emotions that affect our lives today. We can use them as focal points to clear and release outmoded thinking. Then we can release the triggers with ease.

49 **Be aware of body sensations.** Ask your higher self, heart or body part what the sensation is communicating to you. This may lead you to further clarity regarding a past experience.

50 **Take notes of dreams, impressions, and even partial glimpses of memory.** Getting these out of your mind and on paper will give you mental and emotional space to remember more. As you remember more, these puzzle pieces of your past will become more coherent to you.

51 **Tell yourself or your inner child that the experiences in the memory are not happening to you now.** Open your eyes to see that the abusers are not in the room with you now. Know that you are safe from that old experience.

52 **Feel the feelings that you would have felt in the past experience if you had been free to do so.** This will help you put the memory in proper perspective in relation to your whole life. This will take the charge off of the intensity of the memory, particularly if it is new to your conscious mind.

53 **Direct your mind to reveal your memories at a time that is supportive to you.** Simply tell your mind and heart to inform you of new memory information when you are in a therapy session or group, with a supportive friend, on your day off from work, during your meditation time, while journaling or when you consciously choose to feel, listen or see the memory. If you keep your promise to consciously receive the information at those times or in the ways that you designated, your mind will probably cooperate with you by revealing the memory while you are in those supportive conditions.

54 Ask to know only what you need to know. You can let go of the rest. Address your dynamics, lessons, patterns, feelings, emotions, and decisions you made based on the incident. You do not need to figure out other people's motives, issues or actions—only your own.

55 Be very gentle with yourself during the memory recovery process. Since you may experience your thoughts, emotions, and energy in present-time as if you had just been abused, treat yourself as you would a friend who had just been raped. Being kind to yourself now is critical to your healing and the antidote to past abuses.

Write Your Own Ideas Here

_____

_____

_____

_____

_____

5

Re-parenting Your Inner Child

"...Abused children rarely are allowed to be the age they are. They are pressed to face situations that are years beyond their chronological age. So even though your body says that you are an adult, you deserve what every other child deserves. Give it to yourself...and begin to nurture and accept, rather than judge your inner child." Page 297

56 **Pay attention to your inner child.** Spend time with your inner child and be present with him or her. Check in often. Listen and honor messages, needs, desires, and input from your inner child. This can enhance your life immeasurably.

57 **Imagine holding your inner child if s/he wants to be held.** Give gentle, respectful touch and affection. This will heal old wounds and create an experience of healthy touch.

58 **Make up songs together.** This is very empowering, energizing, and uplifting. It opens up a safe, fun, and creative way to be comfortable with verbal communication.

59 **Say kind and loving things to your inner child.** You can correct unhealthy childhood beliefs by reminding him or her of times during any portion of your life when you were successful or had a positive outcome. Talk to your inner child as you wish someone had spoken to you.

60 **Let your inner child know that s/he did not deserve that suffering.** Please know that there is nothing that you could have thought or done to warrant the abusive treatment. You are entitled to be safe and loved and treated with dignity. Even thieves and murderers in prison shun child molesters for having done the most despicable crime.

61 **Make the communication channel 2-way.** Talk and listen. Invite your inner child to do or say whatever s/he wants. Stay open to contact from your inner child even while you are busy with daily life.

62 **Make up a password between you.** Ask your inner child to select any word for your inner child to use to get your attention. Whenever you see or hear this word from the inside or in your physical environment, stop and take a moment to be consciously aware of your inner child.

63 **Be patient with your inner child's needs.** You may be addressing and fulfilling important child developmental stages needed for your growth. Some needs dissolve simply by your being accepting of them.

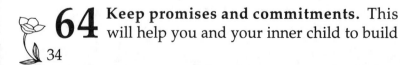 **64** **Keep promises and commitments.** This will help you and your inner child to build

trust and a healthy structure that you can rely on. Consistency is a great security builder to lay a stable foundation. It is a natural contradiction to the inconsistencies and chaos of abuse.

65 Be willing to deal with past hurts, issues, and even suppressed memories of your inner child. This helps you to give your inner child the support necessary to heal and the opportunity to mature emotionally and mentally beyond the years of those fixating experiences of abuse.

66 Believe your inner child. Unlike your abuser, the part of your psyche that your inner child represents has been waiting for you to acknowledge and accept the truth of its experience. This will lead to greater self-acceptance and inner peace.

67 Comfort your inner child. Be gentle with him or her. Your inner child may be constantly reliving the past. Let your inner child know that s/he does not have to go through that experience anymore. In your mind's eye, with your inner child's permission, take him or her out of the old painful environment.

68 Imagine placing your inner child in a safe, joyful place. Some suggestions for this are a treehouse, a beautiful garden or meadow, in your current home, in your heart or with a divine being. This can be done prior to your getting busy with adult activities such as work, having sex, balancing your checkbook or negotiating with other adults on major issues. This will help you focus with your adult mind and avoid sabotage or triggers.

69 **Let your inner child know that it is safe and right to express and release feelings.** Give him or her permission to cry, get mad in a non-destructive way, and tell you anything.

70 **Respect your inner child.** Accept his or her feelings and needs. Use proper pacing and timing when you want information from your inner child. Do not force answers or bombard him or her with questions. Treat your inner child the way you would like to be treated.

71 **Hang out together.** Spend time with your inner child. Get to know each other. Like any good relationship, intimacy will grow in time with proper care and attention. In this way you can cultivate a relationship of love, trust, and joy.

72 **Have fun with your inner child.** Do something that your inner child suggests. This will further awaken a sense of discovery, spontaneity, and joy in your adult life. You can actually do it in the "real" world or you can imagine doing it with your inner child in your mind's eye. Either way you will feel the experience.

73 **Give your inner child the benefit of your life's experience since your childhood.** Your inner child and therefore a part of your psyche may be stuck in the past while the rest of you is many years wiser. Look at your world with fresh eyes. You may now recognize options that you may not have had as a child. Explain to your inner child how your life is different now from when you were a child. Point out the wisdom and freedom of making new choices based on the present moment.

74 **Learn from your inner child.** In some ways your inner child is closer to your true nature. Listen to your child's intuition and perspective as well.

Write Your Ideas Here

_____

_____

_____

_____

_____

_____

_____

_____

_____

_____

_____

_____

_____

_____

_____

_____

_____

_____

_____

_____

_____

_____

_____

_____

_____

_____

_____

_____

6

Overcoming Stuckness

"After a long siege of flooding memories, disturbed nights, and trying to keep my current life together as I am terrorized by my own past, I fall into one of those black holes and I am stuck. The pain of remembering was too excruciating, so I ran from it. My feelings of pain and sadness were then unacknowledged, so part of me got angry. My anger terrified me, so I suppressed it...spiraling down into that black hole."
Page 151

75 Ask yourself, "If I were not feeling stuck now, what emotion would I be feeling instead?" Not feeling this underlying emotion is probably the source of your stuckness. Releasing this underlying emotion will free up your energy and dispel the stuckness.

76 Listen to the negative things that you are telling yourself. Then adopt new or contrary self-talk that supports your life now. If you cannot think of anything positive to say to yourself, imagine what someone who likes or loves you would say, and adopt that for the moment.

77 **Ask why is it that you feel stopped at this time.** What is the message you need to hear? What is the action you need to take that is different from what you have been doing? Perhaps you need to rest, slow down, re-group or need another piece of information to proceed successfully. Perhaps there are old emotions that need to be released so that you can accomplish what you say you want. Listen.

78 **Agree to a processing time.** If you have something that you must do, yet feel stuck, tell the stuck part of you that you will listen to it and work with it at a specific future time. The stuckness will often free up so that you can deal with the present moment effectively. Be sure to sit down with yourself at that specific agreed upon time and deal with the unresolved issue.

79 **Initiate anything.** Begin somewhere. Do one aspect of a task—make a call, touch the papers, write the task on your calendar, pray to God or ask your Higher Self or angels to inspire and support you in accomplishing the task.

80 **Commit to a small unit of time to take action.** Agree to spend just 1, 5 or 10 minutes to be with the feeling or issue that is keeping you stuck— or with the task itself that you feel stuck about doing. You can stop at the end of that time or you may feel unstuck and be inspired to continue.

81 **Educate yourself on the subject to be addressed.** You will feel more comfortable and confident to deal with it. If you do not know what you believe you need to know, get help. If you do know enough to fulfill the task, acknowledge that you have somewhere within you the power, knowledge, courage, strength or whatever quality you need to face the situation.

82 **Envision the task differently than you do now.** See it as something which is supportive when complete or something to accomplish or conquer rather than something to fail at or not enjoy. Rather than imagining yourself in the process of doing the task or facing the feeling, see yourself as having already completed the task and enjoying the benefits that have come of dealing with it.

83 **Empower yourself in the process.** Rather than thinking that someone or some circumstance is making you do something, you can decide to take charge and choose to get it done. Instead of using your power to immobilize yourself, focus that same power toward taking action in a helpful way.

84 **Get out of overwhelm.** Overwhelm can confuse you, immobilize your energy, and block your ability to make clear decisions. See the chapter on overwhelm in this book for some helpful ideas.

85 **Prioritize your tasks.** Base this on your own legitimate life responsibilities and values that enhance the quality of your life experience.

86 **Acknowledge your accomplishments each step of the way, no matter how small they may seem.** As you go along, feel the energy and momentum build toward completion.

41

87 Notice, honor, and work with your natural rhythms. Schedule activities or interactions with others to coincide with your natural flow of energy. Maybe you are more active in the morning or late at night. Maybe you are slow in the morning and feel better in the afternoon—plan accordingly.

88 Use affirmations as healthy reminders, motivators, and to alter unsupportive mindsets. Let the power of the word propel you into action. Create your own affirmations or use the phrase, "There's nothing to it, but to do it."

Write Your Ideas Here

_____

_____

_____

_____

_____

_____

_____

_____

_____

_____

_____

_____

_____

_____

_____

_____

_____

_____

_____

_____

_____

_____

_____

_____

_____

_____

_____

_____

_____

_____

_____

_____

_____

_____

_____

_____

_____

_____

_____

_____

_____

7

Filling Emptiness with Wholeness

"...there grew a great chasm between us. Into this giant abyss fell all my dark thoughts and feelings about myself for never having been received [by my mother]. Through her dismissal of my being, this space became a bottomless pit for all my accruing sense of emptiness." Page 147

89 Realize that feeling empty inside is partly the product of not feeling received or embraced by your parents, the world or life itself. Are they reflecting some part of your consciousness? Check to see if you are not embracing life. Be willing to take life in fully—do not keep it at a distance.

90 Acknowledge your true, divine nature within you. You will feel full of the lightness of your real being. Meditation, contemplation, prayer, journaling, and dialoging with various aspects of yourself will help you get in touch with your True Self.

91 **Fill that seeming emptiness with warm, wonderful qualities.** Visualize that empty space. Then place in it the energies of love, light, joy, clarity, peace, creativity, health, success, freedom, empowerment, confidence, worthiness, wisdom, intuition, abundance, and talents that you wish to express during this lifetime.

92 **Address the fullness of feelings that the empty sensation is masking.** Not feeling the emotions that you do not want to feel may create the illusion of emptiness. Emptiness is really a visceral numbness. It deludes us into thinking that there is nothing of value inside. It is not the truth of your being—it is covering that too.

93 **Re-create through recreation.** Playing games, reading, dancing, sports, and other leisure activities relax your mind and heart. This in turn opens you to the possibilities of re-creating your life as you truly want it.

94 **Stop under-estimating and under-appreciating yourself.** Stop waiting for approval from others. Fill yourself with gratitude, acknowledge your self-worth, and accept who you truly are—over and beyond your abusive past.

95 **Let the sounds out of you that echo your hollow, empty feelings inside.** Scream, cry, yell, and repeat out loud the phrases that rattle around in your head. Really listen to what you release and give them over. Then listen to the peace and quiet that you can now experience inside.

96 **Fill the seeming emptiness with yourself.**
Come home to yourself. It is safe now. The emptiness and longing you feel may be because you have been missing yourself. Ask or pray that the part of you that went away at the time of the abuse, now return home. Allow your true being to fill you and shine through you.

97 **Open to connecting with others.** Look for common interests with others. Join a group of hikers, social activists, musicians or those that mirror any of your interests. As you connect with others in areas other than abuse, there will be room in your heart to connect about more personal subjects. This will relieve your sense of emptiness.

Write Your Ideas Here

_____

_____

_____

_____

_____

_____

_____

_____

_____

_____

_____

_____

_____

_____

_____

_____

_____

_____

_____

_____

_____

_____

_____

_____

8

Dealing with Depression

"Depression is actually a pure act of rejecting everything. It is born out of a suppression of anger which in turn is a separation from an underlying hurt. Depression is a state of rejecting one's own feelings." Page 152

98 **Accept aliveness into your life.** This is a natural contradiction to the rejection of your life that is inherent in the depression. Be around people, animals or nature even if you think that you want to be alone.

99 **Get angry.** Depression can be a suppression of anger. Acknowledging and releasing your anger can shake off a depression. You may feel more empowered. Your fight, passion, and inspiration to heal will return.

100 **Ask yourself, "What am I angry or sad about?"** This simple question is often enough to move you out of the depression and into the awareness of its underlying cause. Yes, it is necessary to feel these underlying feelings with the intention of releasing them.

101 **Move your body.** You will feel better and less depressed in minutes. Your endorphins will circulate and cheer you up. Walk, stretch, jog, play a sport, exercise or put on some music and dance.

102 **Honor your need to grieve your past and the consequences of the abuse on your present.** Honoring allows your anger, pain, sadness, and your sense of loss to move through you for full release. This will create space to experience new possibilities.

103 **Communicate.** Talk about how you feel to another human being. The simple act of talking will move some energy and you will feel lighter even if the problem itself is not yet solved. Call a hotline, friend, therapist, support group, clergyman, radio talk show call-in program or even go to the park and talk to someone who will listen.

104 **Arrange for a friend to hold you in an affectionate, non-sexual way.** This type of touch will help you connect with your own heart in a peaceful, loving, and gentle way. If you cannot find a friend or relative to do this in a way that feels safe for you, you can locate a masseuse or other type of bodyworker who will be willing to do this.

105 **Create a maintenance program of supportive, nurturing activities and agreements with others.** This will help keep you from spiraling into a depression. It gives you a back-up plan to go to at the first signs of depression or something/someone to reach for when you are fully in a depression to help you out of it.

106 **Focus on something outside of yourself.** Sometimes the constant processing of a painful past depresses us. Take a break and do something fun, just for the fun of it.

107 **Straighten up your posture.** If you have been slumped forward, you may wish to arch your shoulders way back in a stretch. Then sit straight without being rigid. This opens up your heart region and your flow of positive energy.

108 **Think about what you would do right now if you were not feeling depressed.** Let the joy of those thoughts flow through you and energize you. Let those ideas inspire you to clear whatever it is you need to clear so that you can do those things.

109 **Get some sunshine.** The warmth, light, and fresh air will lift your spirit.

Write Your Ideas Here

_____

_____

_____

_____

_____

_____

_____

_____

_____

_____

_____

_____

_____

_____

_____

_____

_____

_____

_____

_____

9

Handling Anger

"Anger must be addressed fully so that one can release the pain that resides underneath and return to a heart-based experience of unity and love." Page 170

110 **Focus your anger in the direction it belongs.** By having focused, rather than generalized anger, you can counteract that "out-of-control" fear that often blocks the much needed release of anger. Admit that you are mad at your abusers and/or those who ignored or denied your experience.

111 **Let your release of anger be a truly empowering experience.** As you express your anger, your fear will dissipate. Your confidence and sense of genuine power will increase.

112 **Reclaim your spontaneity and freedom of expression as you release your anger.** Don't let your abuser's prior suppression of your emotions continue to block your natural self. Spontaneity is healthy, uplifting, and natural.

113 **Acknowledge your right to be angry.** Since any type of abuse is a violation of your boundaries, you are entitled and it is natural for you to be angry about it. Stop taking false responsibility for your abuser's inappropriate actions. It is okay to be angry at people whom you also love if they have acted improperly toward you.

114 **Get angry on behalf of your inner child, your childhood or other abused children in the world.** It is often easier to get angry for another's suffering. This will jump-start you on getting comfortable with expressing anger about your own, direct experience.

115 **Tear paper into many tiny pieces.** You can release destructive energy without harming anything. You will feel gratified and relieved of angry tension. Save old phone directories, junk mail and newspapers for your supply. You can still recycle the torn paper.

116 **Draw sprawling scribbles with the colors that best express your anger.** If your anger is big, use big paper. Use a large drawing pad or a roll of shipping or butcher paper. You may find that black, red, and orange are particularly helpful in releasing pent-up anger.

117 **Make sounds that express your anger.** Ask inside what sound speaks your anger. Then mimic or repeat that sound out loud. If you cannot hear or sense that sound, then growl, hiss like a cat, snarl or yell "nnnnnoooooooooooo" or "stop it!" to get your anger release moving.

118 **Stand up for yourself.** Literally stand up and visualize your abusers in front of you. Tell them what they did and how you feel. Tell them that you will not stand for their abuse anymore.

119 **Update your view of your abusers and yourself.** Visualize them at the age they would be now (not how they looked when you were a child). Are they old, feeble or dead? See yourself in your adult body with the strength and resources that you have to protect yourself. You know how to call 911, protect your body, and exercise your legal rights. You probably live elsewhere and those abusers do not have easy access to you. You are free to make your own choices as to whether or not you see them now.

Write Your Ideas Here

_____

_____

_____

_____

_____

_____

_____

_____

_____

_____

_____

_____

_____

_____

_____

_____

_____

_____

_____

_____

_____

_____

10

Diffusing Fear and Panic

"When we feel worthless as a product of abuse, we come to expect further abuse and naturally fear the same. This cycle becomes so strong and reinforced by its own momentum that the distinction between fear and worthlessness becomes a blur. We can become so afraid of being worthless that we set ourselves up for experiences that make us think we are."
Page 231

120 **Shift the way you breathe.** Focus your mind completely on your chest cavity, heart chakra, and your breath. Then alter your breath pattern by breathing slowly and deeply. This will instantly calm your feelings of fear or a panic attack.

121 **Consciously unravel your link between feelings of worthlessness and fear.** One way to begin this process is by realizing that your true worth has nothing to do with the way a disturbed abuser treated you.

122 **Develop your intuition.** This will help you to perceive the truth in the present accurately. You can bypass veils of fear from unresolved past incidents that have been distorting your view. You will also know when the sense of fear in the present is an accurate signal to protect yourself.

123 **Choose to know.** Since most fear is based on not knowing or keeping one's awareness in the dark, visualize shedding light on that which you do not know or understand clearly. Ask questions, access more information or get emotional support to muster the courage to know what you need to know. You may or may not like what you learn, but your fear from not knowing will dissolve.

124 **Ask where this fear signal is coming from.** Dialogue with the fear directly. Ask it if it has a message for you from the past or is it truly about the present circumstances—or both. After you have received the message from the fear, ask that this fear signal cease. If you are being triggered in the present but it is really about the past, negotiate a suitable time to deal with the past issue.

125 **Identify what fear-based decisions you made a long time ago.** Make a list of your negative beliefs. As you do this, make a note of which ones bring up a feeling of fear. Ask when was this belief first created. As you release your feelings from that past incident, you will be able to recognize that you made a decision then that has become a belief you live by now. When you are ready, objectively re-evaluate your fear-based belief. Is this belief really true in all situations with everyone? Is every adult unsafe or untrustworthy? Can you think of even one person in your lifetime who is safe or trustworthy?

Was this global belief initially based on the experience with one abuser or one specific group of people? Update your old belief to reflect the truth in the present.

126 **Honor your fear messages based on specific acquired knowledge.** For example, if you know that a specific person abused you or another in the past, do not override your fear message when you see that person simply because they are acting nice now. Or if you see certain cult symbols or activities that you recognize from prior experience or study as being harmful, accept that your fear message rising up is an added signal to take precautionary action. Others may not agree with you because they have not had direct access to the same information as you have had. Trust what YOU know.

127 **Balance your hyper-vigilance and your sensitivities with the actual need to know.** At a time when you are feeling trusting, safe, confident, and peaceful, ask that you only be signaled for what you truly need to know for your safety and well-being. This can minimize your jumpy, reactivity to every subtle shift in your environment. With practice you will feel safe and more peaceful.

128 **Get mad at your abuser.** Feel your anger. It can burn off your fear and powerlessness. Through visualizing, role playing or journaling, tell your abusers that you are not willing to be a victim—that they have no power over you anymore.

129 **Minimize nightmares, disruptive flashbacks, and insomnia.** You can do this by setting up specific times and supportive situations to deal with fearful issues. Address your fear or your mind by telling it that you will face what it has to communicate to you when you are with a therapist, or supportive friend, when you are journaling or perhaps at a time of day or evening when you have the time, spaciousness, and strength to deal with it.

130 **Take care of yourself.** You may have noticed that fear arises more often or you feel more vulnerable when you are tired, stressed or have agreed to do something that you instinctively knew was not right for you to do. Nurture yourself, get plenty of rest, stay out of high-stress situations when possible, and honor your own wishes.

131 **Strengthen your energy field and raise your vibration.** When your physical vitality is high and your aura is broad you will not live in fear. Some ways to achieve this are to: exercise your body or play a sport, do breathing exercises that better oxygenate your body and your chakras, meditate, do tai chi, chi gung or yoga, clear and balance your chakras, think and say positive affirmations, have fun, laugh, pray or visualize white light moving through you and radiating in all directions beyond you. When you feel physically stronger, more expansive, spiritually connected, and happier, you reduce or dissolve fear.

Write Your Ideas Here

_____

_____

_____

_____

_____

_____

_____

_____

_____

_____

_____

_____

_____

_____

_____

_____

_____

_____

11

Tempering Suicidal Urges

"...to get through the unbearable moment that is evoking a suicidal urge, one needs only to think of a reason to live. Any reason will do, even if it is only to postpone suicide long enough to take out the trash so that those who find you will not remember you as a slob. It does not matter how minuscule or temporal the reason for delay, because an energy in motion tends to remain in motion and will therefore propel you to find another reason to live, and another, and another. The edge of the crisis may ease, or you will simply tire and slumber into a new day in which you have regained tolerance for all you are facing." Page 211

132 **Wait.** Agree not to take action on your suicidal urge today. See how you feel the next day. You may feel a little less stressed, less tired, less destructive. You may feel glad about your choice to wait.

133 **Talk to someone.** Call a hotline, doctor, therapist, friend or human services agency listed in the front section of your local phone directory. Talking will take the edge off of your self-destructive urge.

134 **Vent your anger and your pain.** This will support you in doing what you really need to do rather than destroying yourself in an attempt to destroy the pain and anger inside of you. Let yourself feel and release these feelings.

135 **Find even one thing that you like or love about yourself or the world.** Focus your thoughts and feelings on something or someone in this world that you do care about.

136 **Realize that what you do not face on earth you will take with you.** There is no true escape from what happened to you or your feelings about those events. There is only dealing with them. Suicide will only increase your suffering.

137 **Draw your suicidal urges on paper.** What does it look like? What shape and color is it? What image expresses how you feel? Get this energy out of your body, heart, and mind. Then destroy the paper instead of yourself. Tear, burn, cut or wad up the paper with the drawing and throw it away.

138 **Activate your heart center (heart chakra).** Take a deep breath in your nose. On the exhalation, chant the mantra, "Om" for as long as you still have air. Do this several times until you feel your energy field expand. Another helpful tip is to rest your hand, palm open, on your chest. Then move it in a circular motion several times in a clockwise direction. (As you look down at your hand on your chest, it should be moving against your body in the same direction that a clock hand moves.) This will help you open your heart center. An open heart cannot kill.

139 Read poetry. Poetry has an amazing way of opening your heart quickly and easily. As your heart opens, even if you cry, you will soon feel more spaciousness to deal with whatever has burdened you. You will feel lighter, stronger, and more willing to live.

140 Place yourself around lively activity even if you don't think that you want to right now. Be around people. Go to a park. Go to a movie theater. Come in contact with animals or nature. Do not isolate yourself at this time.

141 Ask the parts of you that DO want to live to write a helpful letter to you. This may come by asking your heart or your Higher Self or a clear aspect of your mind. Then sit down and take dictation from those parts of your consciousness. Simply listen and write what you hear or sense. Then read this letter to yourself. You will be reading the loving truth about yourself.

142 Ask your inner healer to come forward and consciously work in your life now. The famous poet Kahlil Gibran wrote, "Pain is the pill that cracks open the inner physician." Simply ask, "Inner healer, whoever or wherever you are, come forth now. Please assist me now to heal my pain so that I may live in joy." You may then visualize this being or sense its presence. Follow its counsel.

143 Make yourself laugh. Rent a funny video, read the cartoon section of the newspaper, read a joke book, watch a silly sit-com or cartoon on television. This will break your cycle of suffering long enough to help you gain a healthier perspective.

65

144
Think of the mess or problems that you would leave for others to deter yourself from suicide. What about the pain you would cause the person who found your body? Think of the karma of leaving a mess for others to clean up. Is your will up-to-date or do you even have one? Are your financial affairs in order?

145
Think of the people who would miss you. Who would you miss and who would miss you? Is this the way you want to leave your relationships? What would happen to your pets, plants, family, lover, friends, possessions?

Write Your Ideas Here

_____

_____

_____

_____

_____

_____

_____

_____

Dispelling Guilt and Shame

"...guilt and shame are simply not the same...Guilt is instilled through externally sourced standards, trickery or internally manufactured judgments. Guilt carries an element of conscious culpability, conscious breach of conduct, conscious awareness of wrongdoing...Normal human shame arises out of doing or witnessing that which is unnatural or through exposure to that which inherent modesty prompts us to conceal...There is another kind of shame, unhealthy shame. It results from having one's natural boundaries violated...and becoming enmeshed with the shameful thought or behavior imposed." Page 383

146 **Reclaim and honor your awareness of genuine right and wrong conduct.** Realize that your abuser schemed, initiated, tricked, lied, manipulated, coerced, and forced you into abusive situations. Acknowledge that it was your abuser, not you, who acted improperly.

147 **Discern where responsibilities should be.** Is it with your abuser, with you or both? Remember that you are not responsible for another's actions. It is not your fault that they chose you to victimize. If you had not been in that time and place, someone else would have been abused.

148 Realize that it is normal to experience a mixture of feelings about an abuser. This is a person from whom you may have wanted and expected love, approval, and attention. Honor both your feelings of love and your feelings of sadness, anger, disappointment, abandonment, and betrayal.

149 Release your judgments that hold guilty feelings in place. Stop making yourself wrong for the wrong actions of your abuser. Think of children you know or look at children walking in a mall who are the same age as you were when you were abused. Would you judge those children as you have judged yourself? Or would you understand that it would not be their fault if someone were to abuse them?

150 Feel and release your imploded anger. This will help to discharge your feelings of and attachment to guilt.

151 Give up the idea that you should be punished. You can help stop the cycle of violence toward you and others by letting go of trying to punish yourself or others.

152 Feel your remorse to alleviate any guilt. If you truly believe that you have done something wrong, feel your genuine regret for any pain you may have caused, apologize in thought or action, forgive yourself, and vow never to do it again.

153 Untangle your personal identity from the shameful acts performed by your abuser. The abuse that you experienced is not who you are. The shame of that abuse is your abuser's unacknowledged shame, not yours. There is much more to your being than the abuse you endured.

154 Know that you are not bad or flawed. What your abusers did was bad. You lived through a bad situation and are healing from that experience. You may *feel* "bad" or pained—and it is also true that *you* are not bad.

155 Feel, grieve, and release the pain underneath the shame. This will help you heal beliefs of worthlessness and non-deserving of good. This will help you to restore your awareness of your self-worth.

Write Your Own Ideas Here

_____

_____

_____

_____

_____

_____

_____

_____

_____

_____

_____

_____

_____

_____

_____

_____

_____

_____

_____

_____

_____

_____

_____

13

Resolving Abandonment

"Our sense of self-worth is invariably jostled when feelings of abandonment surface. This is because we had an expectation or reliance that rested outside of ourselves. We were therefore attempting to fulfill a need that we perceived we could not satisfy from within. Consequently, when the external supplier of that need leaves...we are left with our own perceived inability to fulfill our own need." Page 291

156 **Stay present with yourself.** Where we cannot be present or give to ourselves is the same area that others may appear to walk away from us. You will not feel abandoned if you do not abandon your hopes, dreams, desires, intentions, goals, heart, inner child and Higher Self.

157 **Seek within yourself what you were wanting from another.** Love, approval, recognition, acknowledgment, understanding, and joy are all things that we can give to ourselves even when someone else cannot seem to give these qualities. In this way, you do not abandon yourself and will feel much better about yourself.

158 Maintain your conscious connection with a divine presence. Pray, meditate or contemplate with God, Jesus, Buddha, Brahma, Quan Yin or any other spiritual form. This will help you to be aware that you are never alone. It will support you in feeling okay with yourself.

159 Detach your sense of self-worth from someone else's boundary choice or unconscious limitation. Realize that their being or not being able to show up in the way that you want them to is about them, not you. You are still lovable and worthy even if someone else cannot recognize this truth or has set a different intention for himself or herself.

160 Look to see if there is an abandonment pattern in your life. Then look to see what your contribution is to it. Do you expect it? Do you attract or are you attracted to people who are quick to abandon? Do you push away or subtly encourage abandonment? Do you abandon first? How might you work with your answers to help yourself in the future?

161 Ask yourself, "What part of myself have I abandoned in this situation?" Perhaps it is your love of self, your creativity, your values or your intuition. Spend time with that part to get re-acquainted. Dialogue with it. Integrate this part with your life's activities by honing that skill, paying more attention to it or reprioritizing so that you somehow include it more.

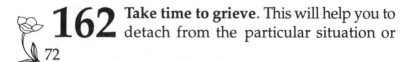

162 Take time to grieve. This will help you to detach from the particular situation or person. You will not lose your memories nor the value you received from that relationship. Grieving will make space for new opportunities to manifest.

163 Ask yourself some questions to shift from victimization to empowerment. Were you negating your own abilities in the situation? Were you taking another for granted? Were you coasting? Were you letting someone else be responsible for your responsibilities? What do you want to do for yourself now to be empowered?

164 Go deeper. Abandonment is often an invitation to find resources within yourself. View this situation as an opportunity for a new adventure. Dive in and enjoy new levels of your self-exploration.

165 Trust that you can move on. Sometimes others play the role of kicking us out of the nest. Sometimes they appear to leave first when it actually was our time to leave. Discover the hidden gift in their leaving. Are you finding your own strength or ability as a result of your doing for yourself what they used to do for you? Recognize your own growth or readiness to move along your life's path.

166 Thank the other person involved. Take time to appreciate what you have learned from the relationship thus far. Know that you may still realize and learn things from having known them long after they are out of your daily life experience. Gratitude will help you receive the gift of the other person having been in your life for the time that they could be there.

Write Your Ideas Here

_____

_____

_____

_____

_____

_____

_____

_____

_____

_____

_____

_____

_____

_____

_____

Boosting Self-Esteem

"It has been my practice to carefully remove insects from the house rather than kill them. Yet as I recovered memories and the accompanying feelings of torment, I often considered killing myself. How little regard I must have had for myself that an insect held greater stature than my own life. How great the impact of abuse can be upon anyone's sense of self-worth." Page 215

167 **Release the devaluating messages or objectification that others imposed on you.** Call forth the stored messages that do not support your experiencing a strong self-esteem. Then visualize releasing them in a way that feels permanent to you. Ask that their energy be transformed into what you want now.

168 **Cancel negative input that does not truly support, serve or teach you something valuable.** Whether it is yourself or another who is telling you something negative, state to yourself that you consciously choose to "cancel" or "not take in" that message. You may wish to affirm that on an ongoing basis, you filter out negative or unhealthy messages at all levels of your being.

169 **Trust that you are lovable.** Know that your abusers did not know how to love themselves or others. Start by loving your inner child who went through the suffering.

170 **View yourself from another point of view.** Imagine that you are one of your friends, a neighbor, a boss or co-worker, a customer, a clerk at a store you frequent or someone else who likes you. What are three nice things that they would say about you?

171 **Realistically re-evaluate what being or not being "good enough" is.** What is its specific quantity or specific scope? Do you truly have a reasonable expectation given your set of life experiences, needs, and interests? Would you expect exactly the same from others? What benefit do you get from judging that you are not "good enough"? Ask your heart for the truth on this whole issue.

172 **Detach from your abuser's humiliating acts and false sense of superiority.** Let go of their actions as a way to define yourself. Feeling humiliated by their cruelty is how you feel but not who you are.

173 **Repeatedly give yourself positive feedback.** Tell yourself things that you do appreciate about yourself. Create affirmations. Thank yourself and take in compliments and gratitude from others. Since we learn through repetition, repeat these positive thoughts to yourself often. It will raise your self-esteem.

174 **Deal with your memories of abuse.** As you unveil your memories, you unmask the sources of your low self-esteem. As you release your feelings related to those memories and reclaim your True Self, your self-esteem will improve greatly.

175 **Join a support group that addresses your issues.** Your self-esteem will strengthen as soon as you are in the company of others who can relate to your experiences. You will get out of thinking that you are crazy or wrong. You will come to feel that what you want to do, say, and feel is just as important as everyone else around you.

176 **Look within yourself to find your lost self-esteem.** Stop gauging your self-worth by standards learned from others. Realize that though you learned many things from your abusers and those in denial around you, they were poor role models. Create your own attainable, healthy standards for yourself.

177 **Create a feeling of accomplishment.** Set yourself up to win or succeed. Select a manageable task and time-frame, commit to it, and follow through as a gift to yourself. You can do this even if it is something that you will be doing for or giving to someone else.

Write Your Ideas Here

_____

_____

_____

_____

_____

_____

_____

_____

_____

_____

_____

_____

_____

_____

_____

_____

15

Redirecting Dissociation

"Dissociation is the mental state of removing one's conscious awareness from associating with or relating to the true present moment ... Along the simple end of its continuum, dissociation can be expressed as a loss of focus or concentration on a project, conversation or thought... [With exposure to] extraordinary volumes or degrees of abuse the child's mind sometimes seeks extraordinary dissociative states as defenses to cope ... At this end of the dissociative continuum we find the defense mechanism of Multiple Personality Disorder [also known as Dissociative Identity Disorder]." Page 93

178 **Choose to be present.** When you notice that you have dissociated or gone away, make a conscious effort to pay attention to the present-time situation. Also, set intentions or pray that you always remain present.

179 **Notice what triggered your wandering away.** This awareness will help you to stay more present next time. What was said? Was it a particular gesture, facial expression, odor, touch or tone of voice? Was it an object in your view or the location you were in? What else might it be?

180 **Notice where you wandered to in thought.** Ask what association does this tangent thought or feeling have to do with the trigger that sparked your dissociative state. They are probably much more connected than you might think.

181 **Look to see what you are protecting yourself from.** Are you avoiding your own feelings? Are you avoiding the emotions being expressed by others? Are you not wanting to hear what they have to say? Or is the other person verbally violating your boundaries?

182 **Look to see what you are protecting from others.** Are you hiding your spontaneity, light or True Self? Are you protecting a talent, gift or skill from being tampered with by others? Are you acting invisible to protect your body? See if you can create other ways to take care of what you want to protect without dissociating. Or perhaps it is time now to expose and use what you have been hiding.

183 **View your experience from a place of oneness or wholeness.** In this way you can simultaneously experience the present situation as well as your trail of thoughts and feelings as being associated with the moment.

184 **Give yourself permission to be spontaneous.** Practice expressing your thoughts and feelings as soon as they arise in the company of safe, understanding people. Build tolerance to your own feelings and memories by exploring them—then you won't feel the need to go away from them.

185 **Communicate with your fears.** Ask, "What part of me is afraid of _____?" Then dialogue with that part of yourself. Let it know what safe and positive changes have happened in your life since the fear was first created. Perhaps you live far away from your former abuser. Perhaps s/he is dead. Perhaps you are an adult and have healthier ways of protecting yourself now.

186 **View dissociation as a linking of two or more unconscious associations.** Dissociation can be like a bread crumb trail that leads you back to a lost part of yourself. Find your buried treasures through this coping mechanism. Then the need to dissociate will dissolve.

187 **See Chapter 13 of** *Abused Beyond Words* **for dissociative issues specifically related to Multiple Personality Disorder or Dissociative Identity Disorder.** In this chapter, you will find information on the various types of personalities and numerous ways to work with them to keep you present, harmonious, and in control. This chapter will also help you heal self-sabotage issues.

188 **Pay attention.** Find ways to stay interested in the conversation or activity. If you are bored or uncomfortable, either check inside yourself to see what is making you feel this way (so that you can stay present) or make a conscious choice to change what you are participating in.

189 **Develop your ability to concentrate.** You can do this by enhancing a skill in sports or other goal-oriented activities, practicing meditation or working on an enjoyable project. You can also do this by cultivating your listening skills or focusing on an object to notice how many details you can discover about it through all of your senses.

Write Your Ideas Here

16

Addressing Addictions and Compulsions

"Since what we resist persists, our addictive behavior must become stronger to combat the mounting pressure of what we do not want to see or feel." Page 328

190 **Reduce your emotional overwhelm.** By feeling your feelings and reducing the excess pressure of overwhelm, you will reduce your need to fulfill your addiction. You will feel better able to cope with daily life.

191 **Stop judging your addiction of choice.** Negative self-talk actually adds to your pain and therefore propels you further in the direction of your addiction or compulsive behavior.

192 **Get emotional support.** Addictions are often compensation for lack of emotional support. With support you can face the feelings that control your addiction.

193 **Know that change from an addictive or compulsive state is possible.** While addiction is in part about control and resisting change, the phenomenal world shows us that at every turn, change is both constant and natural. Focus on your true nature and your addictive desires will dissolve.

194 **Empower yourself.** Acknowledge that you are not the powerless child that was vic-timized a long time ago. Focus on your strengths, creativity, and your apparent ability to adapt. Use these skills to support healthy lifestyle changes.

195 **Focus on the source not the symptom.** If you deal with the thoughts and feelings and issues that you are trying to mask, the symptom (the addiction) will be easier to let go of. You will also develop a genuine control of your life.

196 **Develop relationships with people rather than substances.** Relate more intimately with others by opening up your heart. Share more deeply about yourself and cultivate an interest in others as well.

197 **Use your addiction or compulsion to clue yourself to the specific issue you are covering up.** Do you compulsively shop to buy something of worth as a contradiction to feeling unworthy? Do you use food to control what goes in your mouth to counteract memories of forced oral sex? Do you watch too much television to block out the sight and sounds of a painful past that would otherwise come to mind? Ask how your deeper reason and use of your addiction specifically relates to what you do not want to remember or feel.

198 **Check to see if your addictive survival mechanism is truly supportive to you in present time.** Is it really keeping you safe or is it now unsafe for you physically, emotionally, mentally, spiritually, ethically or legally? Is it enhancing your life or destroying it? Is it a mature or an immature approach to dealing with your issues? Are you controlling it or is it controlling you?

199 **Attune to your heart chakra or sixth chakra or Higher Self.** Invite these aspects of your being to support you and guide you toward healthier ways of living. Then listen, see, feel or perceive what they are communicating to you. Act upon that guidance. Stop blocking out these loving, supportive messages with your addictive acts.

200 **Pray for help.** Seek help from a higher power. Then remember that you have asked for help and accept it when it shows up in your life—even if it is not in the form that you expected.

Write Your Ideas Here

_____

_____

_____

_____

_____

_____

_____

_____

_____

_____

_____

_____

_____

_____

_____

_____

_____

_____

_____

_____

Making Sex Feel Safe
and Loving

"Passion is the feeling that inspiration sparks when it contacts its rightful place in our hearts. It is an expression of the life-force when its flow is unobstructed." Page 367

201 **Take your time.** Healthy relationships evolve over time. You have a lifetime to explore and discover more about each other and yourselves. You do not need to rush things to keep a good partner.

202 **Make agreements in advance that help you to feel safe and comfortable.** For example, you may want to establish verbal or non-verbal signals to acknowledge that you are being triggered or need to stop instantly. You may want your partner to ask for and receive permission from you before touching certain places on your body or doing certain acts with you.

203 **Know that you have the right to stop at any moment.** You may feel the need to slow down or stop. Just because you started, does not mean that you have to finish. A sensitive, loving, understanding partner will accept this without giving you grief, guilt trips or forcing you to do otherwise.

204 **Do only what you truly want to do.** You have every right to stay in control of your body and your choices. A person who loves and respects you will not press you to do otherwise. Remember to love and respect yourself—don't force yourself to do what you do not want to do.

205 **Relax into your own body first.** This will help you stay grounded and present. In this way you can be guided by your body's natural instincts. You can better relate to the other person in real time rather than through filters from the past.

206 **Communicate your wants and needs directly.** No one should be expected to read your mind. (Besides, would you really want that invasion of your privacy?) It is a way to declare what is true for you and to be responsible for the direction of your life. Simply state how you feel and what would be supportive or enjoyable to you. Be honest without manipulating the other person. S/he may or may not be able to accommodate your wishes. But you will know where you stand and can seek other options if necessary. However, if you can ask, it indicates that you are better prepared to receive what you want in this situation or elsewhere.

 207 **Be in the present, not the past.** If you get triggered, acknowledge it to your partner so that you can receive support in the present and keep your communication channels open. Do not withdraw into your private past. This will only isolate you from your partner and your feelings of love. Instead, look into your partner's eyes so that you can distinguish the love available to you in the present from the fear, pain or torment of the past.

208 **Be tender with each other in words, actions, thoughts, and touch.** Treating each other with care and consideration cultivates a sense of safety, trust, and respect. In turn, this leads to greater intimacy and joy. You will feel greater self-worth as well as appreciation of your partner. Additionally, it is a great healing contradiction to an abusive past.

209 **Consider sharing from your loving hearts rather than acting out objectifying fantasies.** Fantasies are mental stimulus to compensate for a lack of emotional intimacy. By engaging in fantasy acts, you will feel less safe and be engaging in dynamics that are reminiscent of past abusive activity. Heart-based sexual relating will support you to feel safer, more trusting, and open with each other.

210 **Be affectionate with touch in non-sexual ways as well.** This nurtures the heart and deepens your love for one another. This will increase a sense of security, balance, and intimacy in your overall relationship. You will feel safe to be close without feeling compelled to be sexual. You will not need to pull away from your partner because you fear that any touch will automatically have to lead to sex.

Write Your Ideas Here

_____

_____

_____

_____

_____

_____

_____

_____

_____

_____

_____

_____

_____

_____

_____

18

Deepening Your Awareness
with Questions

*Asking questions from a variety of perspectives will broaden
your awareness of your situation. The following questions
will help you to uncover underlying conflicts, recognize
dynamics that are causing repeat experiences, and focus on
inner sources of the cause rather than outer symptoms,
catalysts or triggers. If any answer you receive is unclear
to you, ask for clarification. Please do not use any answer to
judge or beat up on yourself. Simply ask a follow-up question
such as, "How can I heal this or move through this?" or
"What supportive act could I take to empower myself in
this situation?"*

211 **"What is my role in this situation?"**
—upper hand or victim, feeling powerful
or powerless, aware or in the dark...?

212 **"What emotion is being surfaced or
cleared by this situation?"** Check your
past to find the original source of this reaction.

213 **"What emotion am I resisting feeling?"** Then feel this emotion and its impact on your life. You may wish to ask for support from a higher power, therapist or friend.

214 **"Within the situation, what pattern or dynamic am I replaying?"** How is the pattern familiar to you? Is it time to create a new, healthy, more supportive pattern?

215 **"What belief or judgment is this situation bumping into?"** Look to see what decision you made a long time ago that has become the foundation of this current belief or judgment. Is this decision still appropriate for your present life? Can you alter this decision now? Would it help you to do so?

216 **"What would I have to be thinking about myself or others to be in this situation in the way that I am?"** The world reflects to you what you believe. Perhaps some part of you feels that you are bad, worthless or not good enough. You may have conflicting thoughts co-existing such as, "I deserve to be treated better than that" and "I deserve to be punished." Or, "No one understands me" and "I don't care what anyone else thinks."

217 **"Did I see this coming but not listen to myself?"** All beings are intuitive. The difference is that some choose to listen to and act upon the messages they receive, while others dismiss them. Practice trust by trusting your own intuition.

218 **"How am I attracting this situation into my life?"** Are you being too open or not open enough? Explore what thoughts and feelings are creating an environment in which this experience can live and grow?

219 **"What message or lesson am I to learn from this?"** Even though something may be painful or confusing, there is a gift within every experience. If you can receive it, you can move on.

220 **"What outcome am I experiencing or expecting thus far?"** This will clue you to your subconscious expectations and beliefs that are influencing the situation.

221 **"What other outcomes can also occur?** This is not a fear-based question. Imagine that your answer is based on having no limitations. Be positive. Be creative. Be receptive to a great outcome.

222 **"What can I learn from what other people are creating?"** If you like what others are creating for themselves, then let them mentor you. Observe them. Listen to their view of life. If possible, ask them questions. Place yourself in the company of success, not failure.

223 **"What outcome do I really want?"** Give yourself permission to have what you want. Then ask your heart or Higher Self questions that will promote manifesting what you want.

224 **"How can I create what I really want without harming, taking advantage of, or being disrespectful to others?"** All things are mutual. If you are being honest with and respectful of yourself, then what you want will ultimately be right for all concerned.

93

225 **"What are my thoughts about God in relation to this situation?"** Your personal view of divinity directly affects your life experiences. If you believe that God abandoned you, you will experience abandonment in many situations. If deep down you believe that Spirit is abundant and generous, you will experience prosperity in your life.

226 **"Is my faith intact?"** Look to see where you place your faith—in other people's desires and values, in the false beliefs of yourself or others, in your ego, in your own heart or in a divine source? How does where you place your faith influence your life?

227 **"What goal is this situation related to?"** Your goal may be a decision, desire, or expectation set a long time ago or recently. It may be the result of a new change in your viewpoint, values or sense of self-worth. It may be integral to your life purpose. Explore what it is for you.

228 **"Am I clearing an obstacle to this or another goal?"** Sometimes seeming adversity is simply helping you dissolve blockages to what you say you truly want. Realizing this can help you work with the situation rather than fight it (and yourself).

229 **"How would God, Divine Mother or Buddha view this situation?"** Using a divine presence as a focal point can help you see your situation from a much broader perspective. It can give you ideas that you might not have thought of otherwise.

230 "How does my Higher Self view this?" Your soul knows the best way for your life path. Invite it to light your way and follow its guidance.

231 "Is there another possible outcome known or unknown to me?" This question stretches your mind and heart. It helps you to allow yourself to entertain other options.

232 "What does God, my Guardian Angel, Higher Self, Soul, and Heart want for me?" (Ask one aspect at a time.) This is a way to attract awareness of your highest good. It also brings your will into harmonious alignment with all levels.

233 "What do I really want for myself now?" Ultimately the decision is yours as to how you live your life. Use your free will wisely. Yet know that true free will is such that what you want in your heart of hearts is the same as what divinity wants for you. Listen to your heart.

234 Ask your heart or Higher Self, "What is the truth of this situation?" The answers will be simple, straightforward, and honest. Your heart and soul will tell you what you need to know.

235 "How can I resolve _____ or make peace with it now?" Answers, messages or solutions are always within the problem itself. Dialogue with the issue itself for greater clarity.

236 "What is my next step?" Implement the answer you receive and then ask this question again to receive the next step, and the next...

95

Write Your Ideas Here

_____

_____

_____

_____

_____

_____

_____

_____

_____

_____

_____

_____

_____

_____

_____

_____

19

Moving Beyond Abuse...

"[Survivors] ask the question, 'Why, but why?' as they angrily cry ... Those are the kind of questions that go round and round in the mind like a squirrel in a cage ... It is only when we can stop asking why that we can settle into our hearts. There we must first do our grieving. We must empty out our suffering to make room for another experience. Then a different kind of answer naturally emerges. It is one of peace." Page 405

237 **Nurture yourself on an ongoing basis.** Let go of treating yourself as your abusers once did. You not only deserve to be treated well, it is your natural entitlement. You must also be the first to do so—then the world will reflect this to you.

238 **Give up the idea that it is your job to fix or change others.** You will feel a burden lift. Focus the energy you were applying to others on healing yourself instead.

239 **Decide what is important and what is not at this point in your life.** Re-evaluating your current priorities may change how you spend your time, energy, and money. Besides, does your abuser still deserve so much attention?

240 Focus on what you have learned, gained or transformed from your past abusive experiences. This will help you appreciate the hidden gifts. Your anger will more easily dissolve and you will feel happier.

241 Let go of your desire to punish. That issue is between those who harmed you and their higher power. Your freedom and strength will increase as you detach from monitoring your abusers.

242 Let go of expecting others to be where you are in awareness. They may not have had your same intense motivation to heal nor the opportunity to receive therapy or other support focused on the subject of abuse.

243 Accept where others are in awareness without judging them. They are more likely to open to what you have to share if you are accepting of them. Defenses rise up and tolerance backs down when people feel judged.

244 Identify your life lessons from the abuse and from your healing process. Then let these lessons guide you to fulfill your calling, mission or service to benefit yourself and others. Let the wisdom you gained enhance the quality of your life and that of those around you.

245 **Live in the present.** Be aware of who you are now. You are no longer a helpless child. You are a survivor with many strengths. You can make life choices that support your well-being now.

246 **Decide for yourself what you want.** Even if your life now is not exactly the way you want it, be honest with yourself and decide how you want it in the future. Next, commit to your decisions. Then ask for guidance as to how to manifest it one step at a time. Be sure to watch for signals and opportunities appearing in your life. Seize them!

Write Your Ideas Here

_____

_____

_____

_____

_____

_____

_____

_____

_____

_____

_____

_____

_____

_____

_____

_____

_____

_____

_____

_____

_____

_____

_____

_____

_____

_____

20

Cultivating Compassion

"Compassion is the transformative link between suffering and surrendering on the path to your True Self." Page 420

247 **Embrace Suffering.** Accept suffering in its entirety rather than pushing away at it. This will help you to soften its grip on you. While it usually feels like it, suffering is not your enemy. It is the message bearer showing you the obstacles in consciousness to your goals.

248 **Cease judging yourself and others.** To reach the loving heart of compassion, it is necessary to release the mental activity of judgment. When you judge, you feel separate from that which you judge. When you are compassionate, you feel accepting and connected with yourself and others.

249 **Learn to deeply feel and express your feelings without judgment.** Feeling deeply is achieved through building tolerance to unwanted feelings. Pace yourself; do not push yourself. Be gentle with yourself.

250 **Accept your full range of feelings.** Neither shy away from joy nor problems. This is part of accepting the human condition and having compassion for your process of healing. This will dissolve your empty feelings and replace them with an experience of fullness and wholeness.

251 **Feel reverence for your life.** Honoring the road you have taken to get to where you are opens you to compassion. It helps you learn your lessons and deepen your wisdom.

252 **Place yourself in the company of compassionate people.** Feeling their compassion will help you to feel safe and build your courage and confidence. This will help mentor and awaken your own capacity to be compassionate toward that which you have found difficult to accept.

253 **Be present and open-hearted.** Be a good listener. Be attentive. Be quiet inside. Compassion is not about doing. It is an open-hearted state of being.

254 **Release your grief.** Empty your heart of your emotions and you create room to restore the heart to its natural state—that of love. You will feel open, light, and spacious—qualities of compassion.

255 **Be gentle with yourself at all levels.** Be kind to your body with healthy foods, non-abrasive exercise, and loving touch. Allow your feelings to flow without reprisal. Relax your mind. Get in touch with your spirit.

256 **Deny nothing.** In this way there will be nothing left to suffer over. Be honest with yourself every step of the way.

Write Your Ideas Here

_____

_____

_____

_____

_____

_____

_____

_____

_____

_____

_____

_____

_____

_____

_____

_____

_____

_____

_____

_____

_____

_____

_____

_____

_____

_____

_____

Exploring Spiritual Tools

"While many tools herein are original in design, this book also offers practical tools drawn from my experience of many psychological and spiritual disciplines. Such teachings and insights are not intended to sway people away from or toward any spiritual tradition. They are simply being shared for their inherent wisdom, healing, and potential for creating peace." Page 3

257 **Consciously connect with God, Christ, your Buddha Nature or your Higher Self to light your way through your healing process.** Invite them to be present with you during your therapeutic work, whenever you are remembering an upsetting event or whenever you get triggered. This makes dealing with dark, heavy issues easier, clearer, less painful, and less time-consuming.

258 **Ask for inner guidance fully.** When you do not understand some image, word or sensation that comes to you as a message, ask for further clarity. Ask that it come to you in a way that you can consciously understand.

259 Pray, let go of the prayer, then pay attention. Remember what you have prayed for. Accept reasonable forms of help along the way even if they are a little different than the form you prayed for. Listen to inner guidance, notice what comes, be receptive, and give thanks for it.

260 Clear your reactive emotions so that your intuitive feelings will register consciously in your heart. Emotions are distorted, reactive energy whereas feelings are intuitive messages. As you clear old emotional baggage, your discernment of intuitive messages will increase.

261 Act upon your inner guidance or new awareness. This helps ground your insight to integrate it in your life and conscious experience. It is important to "walk your talk".

262 Meditate on your true nature. This will help you dispel the false beliefs you adopted about yourself and others from having been abused. It will also bring forth your strength and trust of your own perceptions to deal with difficult aspects of your healing process.

263 Practice mental and meditative control over your emotions, triggers, and negative thoughts. This means to use the awareness, centeredness, and calm that are cultivated by your meditative practice and then be in or apply that peaceful state to these other states mentioned. The result is that you will be less reactive, more in control over your responses, and be able to dissolve negative thinking that lowers your energy and sabotages your life.

264 Learn how to clear your chakras (energy centers along the spine that interface with the endocrine system and non-physical dimensions). You will feel more balanced, centered, and joyful, and function better on a daily basis. Your healing will take less time and be more profound.

265 Create a mantra to support you in some way. Pick a word, such as "peace" or a phrase from a known prayer that brings you calm, hope or some other feeling you seek. Say it to yourself often to engrain it in your brain. Then when you need it, this thought will come to you automatically.

266 Do a practice that promotes conscious harmony of your body, mind, heart, and spirit. Yoga, tai chi, and chi gung are excellent examples of such practices. For instruction, take a class, watch a video or read a book on the subject.

267 Focus on and attune to your limitless (divine) nature. This will help you to dissolve old feelings of limitation. It will increase your abundance in many areas of your life.

268 Accept change and growth rather than resist it. This is a natural part of your spiritual evolution. Honor all reflections of divinity as they manifest in various forms.

269 Remember that responsibility comes with maturity. Responsibility is not a burden. It is a privilege. It is the ability to respond clearly in the present. From a spiritual perspective, you know that you are never alone with any responsibility. Spirit is with you always.

Write Your Own Ideas Here

_____

_____

_____

_____

_____

_____

_____

_____

_____

_____

_____

_____

_____

_____

_____

_____

_____

22

Alternative Healing Methods

The following treatments and practices may support you to release emotions, physical pain, tension, and unblock holding patterns in your body, mind, heart, and spirit. As you feel greater physical vitality, your morale will pick up as well. A very brief description is given for each method. Please consult with a practitioner in the given field for details. Also consult with your doctor and therapist as to which modalities will best complement your healing process for your particular situation. Explore, experience, embrace...

270 **Acupressure and Acupuncture** are branches of Chinese medicine. The practitioner applies either pressure with the fingertips or extremely fine needles to the acupuncture points. This alleviates blockage along the energy pathways called meridians. A licensed acupuncturist may also prescribe Chinese medicine that is composed of various plants, trees, and sometimes animal products. Many types of physical and emotional states can be brought back into balance. These methods can also be used to heal addictions.

271 **Aromatherapy** uses the inhalation of oil essences of various herbs and flowers which have specific healing properties for physical, emotional, and mental states.

272 **Art Therapy** can assist you to draw out your creativity, expressiveness, thoughts, feelings, and memories using various art mediums.

273 **Ayurveda** is an East Indian holistic medical system which addresses the physical, emotional, mental, and lifestyle conditions when diagnosing and treating. These methods are quite different from the Western medical model, yet quite effective. Dietary modification, internal cleanses, herbal supplements, yoga, and oil massage can be part of the treatment program.

274 **Bach (and other) Flower Remedies** are composed of various flower extracts which are ingested or applied to the skin to receive their healing benefits.

275 **Chi Gung** is a practice of movement, inner stillness, breath, and meditation based on Taoist principles. Its purpose is to harness and balance the energies of heaven, earth, and the human being. It promotes health, longevity, and a calm mind.

276 **Chiropractic** is a method of bone manipulation and stimulation of their attachments. It can provide balance, better circulation, freedom from pain, and alleviation of swelling or pressure on nerves which supply messages to the rest of the body. Your disposition and emotional states can also be assisted through this method. The client remains clothed.

277 **Cranio-Sacral** is a bodywork method that works with balancing the rhythm of the spinal fluid and the connective tissue throughout the body. Physical and emotional trauma is stored in the connective tissue. Therefore this work is particularly good for releasing old emotional traumas and physical injuries. The client can remain clothed.

278 **Dance Therapy** uses movement and music to open up expression and shift your unfavorable perceptions of your own body. It can help you to become more fluid in your movements and in your thinking. Your creative juices will come alive.

279 **Exercise** comes in many forms. Choose something that you enjoy so that you will stick with it. Exercise will counteract depression, improve your disposition in general, heal many aches and pains, and channel the release of emotional energy in a constructive way.

280 **Feldenkrais** is a method of movement that teaches you to get in better touch with your body, new ways of holding and moving your body, and how to release pain and tension.

281 **Herbs, Vitamins, and Mineral Supplements** can improve physical, emotional, and mental states by supplementing deficiencies in your diet. Consult a physician, nutritionist or do your own research.

282 Holotropic Breathwork is a guided process using deep breathing and evocative music to reach deeper states of consciousness—consciously. Stuck patterns, previously veiled memories, and emotions are often explored and released through this process.

283 Homeopathy uses natural herb and flower remedies to stimulate the mind and the body's innate ability to heal itself. Mental, emotional, and physical conditions are transformed through this method. You may wish to set up emotional support if you are going to use this system for emotional balancing as you may have a strong releasing experience while you are coming into balance with the desired effect.

284 Jin-Shin works with the energy meridians along the body. The practitioner gently places his or her hands on two points along the energy path and facilitates the movement of energy between those two points. The practitioner then proceeds to the next two points and so forth. This non-invasive bodywork system is great for many physical problems. It can be a gentle, easy path of healing for sexual abuse survivors who find touch difficult. The client usually remains clothed.

285 Massage encompasses many styles and techniques of bodywork to relax and tone muscles and ligaments, aid circulation, and promote the release of toxicity from your body. It can also help trigger or release emotions and memories stored in your body.

286 **Meditation** is a practice of stilling and quieting the analytical mind and opening to deeper perceptions of truth. It can help you to dissolve illusions, emotions, reactivity, and mental chatter. You will feel more peaceful, clear, and centered. Your intuitive guidance will heighten in your conscious awareness.

287 **Myofascial Release** is a form of body-work that massages and manipulates the connective tissue (which stores trauma) throughout the body. It can help release pain, memories, and emotions.

288 **Osteopathy** is a combination of bone and myofascial tissue manipulation. Release of pain and emotions is a common response. The client remains clothed.

289 **Nutrition** can affect not only our physical health, but our emotional and mental states as well. Various foods can promote clear thinking and vitality while others may induce depression, agitation or mood swings. Consult with a nutritionist or do your own research.

290 **Prayer** clarifies and focuses your intentions and sets them in motion. "Ask and ye shall receive" is both an acknowledging and a surrendering spiritual practice.

291 **Reflexology** is used to stimulate points on the hands, feet, and ears which in turn stimulate the body's natural potential for self-healing throughout the psycho-physical system. This non-invasive bodywork system can be a gentle, easy path of healing for sexual abuse survivors who find touch difficult. The client usually remains clothed.

292 **Reiki** uses a spiritual energy system to facilitate healing for the physical and emotional bodies. A light hands-on touch is used and the client remains clothed.

293 **Rolfing** is a systematic process of deep tissue bodywork that also incorporates the use of words. It addresses buried trauma, postural misalignment, held tensions, and pain.

294 **Rosen Method** is a systematic bodywork process using gentle touch and words It concentrates on the release of muscular holding patterns that are storing physical pain and emotions.

295 **Sandtray** is a psychotherapeutic process that uses a small sandbox as the safe, contained arena in which the client places small figures to create a scene. The client uses this to facilitate the discovery of feelings and the telling of his or her story.

296 **Self-Defense Instruction**, whether it be the teaching of modern techniques or any of the many ancient forms of martial arts, can build confidence, improve protection and boundary skills, and move you toward an empowered way of being in the world.

297 **Shen** is a gentle method which focuses on healing your emotional wounds using a light touch and talk through a systematic method of circulating "qi" (also known as "chi" or "life-force" energy) throughout the client's body. This can release old emotions and thereby restore a balanced and empowered state.

298 **Shiatsu** is a Japanese massage technique using acupressure points to relieve pain and tension and to increase circulation and vitality. The client may remain clothed.

299 **Tai Chi** is a fluid series of movements that promotes and emphasizes harmony and health through the flow of chi.

300 **Watsu** is a shiatsu massage that takes place in a pool of warm water. Your body floats as you are gently stretched and massaged.

301 **Yoga (Hatha Yoga)** is the union of body, mind, and spirit through placing the body in specific positions (asanas). It is based on ancient East Indian spiritual teachings. Greater health, flexibility, and peace of mind are achieved with this practice.

You can locate practitioners of these systems by researching health food store and bookstore bulletin boards, schools that teach these methods, your local phone directory, the classified section of newspapers, specialty magazines, the Internet, your local library or by asking your friends and healthcare practitioners for referrals.

Write Your Own Ideas Here

_____

_____

_____

_____

_____

_____

_____

_____

_____

_____

_____

_____

_____

_____

_____

_____

_____

23

Reclaiming Your True Self

"The True Self is you being totally immersed in your humanity as you express your divinity. It is being conscious of your soul in action. It is being Spirit in form. It is being what the Japanese call "makoto"—compassion, wisdom, and integrity all rolled into one. It is the essence of your being."
Page 428

302 **Know that your True Self is not defined by what you do or what has been done to you.** Discover and focus on your eternal being. It is the place in you that is untouched by changing events or reactions to them. See chapter 21, "Exploring Spiritual Tools", for suggestions on getting in touch with this aspect of yourself.

303 **Make a conscious choice to get in touch with the essence of your being.** Make it a priority in your life to meditate, visualize, feel, experience, and listen to your Higher Self, seventh chakra, Christ consciousness, Buddha nature, light within you—or by any other name—your True Self.

304 Take responsibility for your past decision to turn away from your True Self. Ask to uncover the moment in time in which you went away from yourself. Feel the feelings associated with that time and release them. Ask what decisions you made (about yourself, others, God, life or the world) at that time and why. Accept that you made the best choice available to you at that time in consideration of the circumstances and your knowledge then.

305 Make a new choice that supports your True Self expression in daily life now. You may wish to decide that you do not have to hide anymore or that you have worth to share or that you are entitled to shine your light too.

306 Look within for a spark of light. Close your eyes and see (or ask to be shown) your divine spark of light. This will guide you to your True Self.

307 Listen to your heart. Breathe deeply. Open up your chest by stretching. Quiet your mind chatter and focus on your heart. Listen. Your heart speaks the truth to you.

308 Attune to your Higher Self. Focus directly above your head. Visualize white light streaming into you through the top of your head. Sense this presence of your True Self. Perceive its guidance for you.

309 Develop your intuition. Honor your hunches or gut feelings by acting upon them. This will cultivate trust which in turn will help you get more intuitive messages. You will find that your intuition is a direct path to your True Self. (See "Exploring Spiritual Tools"chapter for other ideas.)

310 **Detach from your false identity.** Let go of thoughts that perpetuate illusion, separation, judgment or negative feelings about yourself. Dialogue with your false identity to learn its true message for you. Invite it to retire or give its energy a new job that will be of help to you. Then choose to listen to your True Self instead.

311 **Go to the place where you hid your True Self.** Close your eyes and ask your inner child, heart, Higher Self, or God to guide you to where you went in consciousness to protect yourself. You will find a safe place and your True Self waiting for you there. Invite your True Self to bring its light and love and awareness back to your body now.

312 **Relax.** Know that your True Self is always with you. It is a matter of you consciously realizing this. Rather than efforting, relax and simply pray or invite this truth to become evident to you.

313 **Lower your defenses.** Imagine your anger, sadness, disappointments, and fears dropping away just for now. You will find your True Self under all that.

314 **Get Quiet.** Take a minute, an hour or a day to be completely quiet. Turn off the radio, television, phone, and computer. Do not read, write or journal as these are silent forms of talking.

Do not talk or gesture messages to others. As much as possible, set it up that others do not talk to you. This will give you time for your mind chatter to rise up and settle down. This paves the way to hearing your True Self more clearly.

Write Your Own Ideas Here

_____

_____

_____

_____

_____

_____

_____

_____

_____

_____

_____

_____

Transforming Affirmations

We all learn through repetition. If we are told negative things repeatedly or if we say them silently to ourselves—consciously or subconsciously—we will believe and hold them to be true. The same is true regarding positive statements. Therefore, we can learn to believe positive things about ourselves and bring them into our daily life experience through the repeated use of affirmations.

Affirmations are positive statements phrased in the present tense. Generally, they do not have a negative word such as "not", "none" or "no"—the theory being that the universe does not hear the negative. Yet we do live in a dualistic world of positive and negative—and to simply negate the existence of negatives does not make them go away. True oneness embraces and includes everything, negates nothing. I have found that there are times when the use of such negative words helps turn the tide in thinking from a deeply entrenched negative past experience. Some people who have been abused need to learn to say "no" in a positive way. The first affirmation listed is a perfect example of this.

Use affirmations to reinforce the positive without negating your feelings or covering over problems. The use of "I am" in an affirmation is referring to the nature of your being, not your ever-changing states of feelings and life conditions. How you feel is not the truth of who you are. "I am" is an identifying phrase. It is better not to use it in conjunction with how you feel temporarily, but rather with the underlying positive truth of your eternal nature. This will help you to detach from unpleasant feelings and bring forth your innate potential for joy and peace. Therefore you may say, for example, "I feel fragile at this moment and the truth is, I am a strong and empowered being." Having acknowledged your feelings and by repeating the positive "I am" portion of the statement many times, you may find that the unsettled feelings will dissolve in the light of the whole truth spoken.

You can state affirmations to yourself, write them in your journal or post them on signs in areas where you will notice them. You may even wish to record your affirmations on an audio cassette to listen to before or as you fall asleep, in the morning as you prepare for your day or play it in the car and listen to positive, peaceful, and supportive thoughts as you move through rush hour traffic.

The following affirmations begin with the phrase, "the truth is." You may use or skip this portion of the affirmation. Many of my clients have found that the use of this phrase helps them to consciously resonate more deeply with the part of their being that does know the truth irrespective of their feelings or life conditions. They feel more powerful. Try it to see if it works for you. If not, then simply begin your sentence with, "I am..."

315 The truth is, I am not my abuser's actions.

316 The truth is, I am safe in this moment.

317 The truth is, I am free to make my own decisions now.

318 The truth is, I can trust myself again.

319 The truth is, I live in the present, not the past.

320 The truth is, I am not a child anymore.

321 The truth is, I am an adult now.

322 The truth is, I am strong.

323 The truth is, I am so much more than the suffering that I have experienced.

324 The truth is, I can turn my feelings of vulnerability into tenderness.

325 The truth is, I can release my pain and anger in healthy ways.

326 The truth is, I have learned from my past and can let go of the pain of it now.

327 The truth is, my grief is washing away my old pain.

328 The truth is, I am lovable.

329 The truth is, I am worthy of wonderful treatment.

330 The truth is, I am not responsible for my abuser's thoughts, words or deeds.

331 The truth is, it is not my job to fix my abuser.

332 The truth is, when I listen to my heart, I know that its guidance is right for me.

333 The truth is, I know the truth.

334 The truth is, I am my own being.

335 The truth is, I am now in charge of my life.

336 The truth is, I can be gentle and kind to myself now.

337 The truth is, my discernment is restored.

338 The truth is, I am free.

339 The truth is, I can create a healthy, happy and harmonious life now.

340 The truth is, I choose peace.

341 The truth is, my feelings are appropriate.

342 The truth is, confidence grows within me daily.

343 The truth is, triggers do not have to control me.

344 The truth is, it is safe for me to express myself.

345 The truth is, I now choose to be a fully empowered person.

346 The truth is, I am not a victim anymore.

347 The truth is, I choose to attract wonderful relationships into my life now.

348 The truth is, I choose to be prosperous.

349 The truth is, I choose to be healthy and happy.

350 The truth is, I have access to all of the resources I need to create what I want.

351 The truth is, it is safe for me to open to vitality and love of life now.

352 The truth is, I choose to nurture myself in healthy, joyful ways

353 The truth is, I have survived my painful past.

354 The truth is, I choose to follow my heart.

355 The truth is, there is great kindness within me.

356 The truth is, the past has no hold on me because I have the power to let it go.

357 The truth is, I am who I am.

358 The truth is, as I am loving toward myself, the world reflects that love to me.

359 The truth is, I am consciously guided by the light of truth.

360 The truth is, speaking the truth sets me free.

361 The truth is, I am healing in my own right timing.

362 The truth is, suffering is not eternal.

363 The truth is, I now choose to awaken to my true nature.

364 The truth is, God loves me.

365 The truth is, I decide, God provides.

Write Your Own Ideas Here

_____

_____

_____

_____

_____

_____

_____

_____

_____

_____

_____

_____

_____

_____

_____

_____

_____

_____

_____

For Books, Tapes, Consulting Services & Events
Visit Our Website at: www.pathwaysunited.com
Or Use this Order Form

TITLE   **PRICE**   **QUANTITY**   **TOTAL**

365 Empowering Ways .... $9.95 x _____ = _____

Abused Beyond Words
(Soft Cover) .... $24.95 x _____ = _____

Abused Beyond Words
(Hard Cover) .... $39.95 x _____ = _____

             SUBTOTAL   _____   _____

California Residents add 7.25% sales tax ....   _____

Shipping Charges Within the United States: ....   _____
$4.00 for *365 Empowering Ways* $3.00 each additional of same
$6.00 for *Abused Beyond Words* $5.00 each additional of same
*Shipping Charges Outside of the United States: ...   _____
*Double the Above Fees

         TOTAL.......................   _____

Please Circle Form of Payment: **Check**   **Money Order**
Credit Card: Visa   **MasterCard**   **American Express**

Card #:_____**Exp. Date**_____

Name on Card (please print) _____

Your Signature_____
SHIP TO:
Name_____

Street Address_____

City_____**State**_____ **Zip**_____

Phone (day)_____**(eve)**_____

Fax_____ **E-mail**_____

PLACE YOUR ORDER BY ANY OF THE FOLLOWING:

<u>IN U. S.</u> **CALL TOLL FREE: (877) PUP-1010 • (877) 787-1010**
MAIL CHECK & ORDER TO: Pathways United Publications
P. O. Box 7031 • Corte Madera, CA 94976-7031 USA
OR CHECK OUR WEBSITE FOR OTHER OPTIONS
          www.pathwaysunited.com